Talk to Me 1

2ND Edition

Happy House

Contents

Picture Description

Picture Discussion

Story Making

Debate

Unit	Title	Talking About	Example
01	We Are Playing Together	actions	• The man is writing an email and drinking coffee. • The dog is sleeping on the sofa.
02	Everyone Looks Different	people's appearances	• The girl has long blond hair and brown eyes. She is wearing a blue dress. She looks happy.
03	Shapes Are Everywhere	objects	• My cushion is orange. It is small. It looks like a star. It feels soft and light.
04	I Am Busy Every Day	daily routines	• I wake up at 7:30 in the morning. Then, I go to school with my sister. I eat lunch at noon. After school, I go to English class.
05	Where Is the Sofa?	locations	• There are a sofa, a lamp, a coffee table, and a TV in the living room. The sofa is behind the coffee table. The lamp is next to the sofa. The TV is on the wall.
06	I Love Animals	animals	• A koala has big ears and sharp claws. It lives in trees and eats leaves. It can sleep in trees.
07	Welcome to My Neighborhood	places in a neighborhood	• I go to the post office to mail letters. • I can buy stamps at the post office.
08	Do You Like All Kinds of Food?	likes and dislikes	• I like pizza because I like cheese. I don't like shrimp because I have an allergy to shrimp.

Unit	Title	Talking About	Example
09	That Is What I Need!	things needed to do something	• I need a tent, a campfire, and food for camping. • I'm going camping, so I need a sleeping bag and a cap.
10	Sometimes I Feel Annoyed	feelings	• I feel annoyed when my sister eats my food. I feel sad when it is raining on picnic day.
11	This Is My Family	people around you	• My dad is a police officer. He likes music. My brother is funny, and he is good at art.
12	Let's Imagine!	imaginary situations	• I would fly to Australia. • I would be a superhero and help people.
13	My Pet Is Sick	jobs	• Vets help sick animals. They work at animal hospitals. They wear a uniform. They are very kind.
14	What Will Happen Next?	predictions	• I think lots of scary aliens will come out. • I expect cute and friendly aliens will come out.
15	Let's Twist Fairy Tales!	predictions	• I think the prince will marry the ugly sister. • Perhaps Cinderella will find another prince.
16	Which Side Are You On?	opinions on which is better	• I agree because dogs are more fun and friendlier. • I disagree because dogs are loud but cats are quiet.

How to Use This Book

This section is an introduction to the unit and grabs the attention of the students. It has a focus picture followed by three questions. The questions are either comprehension or conversational and are designed to get students talking straight away. Some of the questions act as a springboard to the rest of the unit.

You Can Say This

This part is directly related to some of the questions above. It gives the students key or example phrases and sentences used throughout the unit.

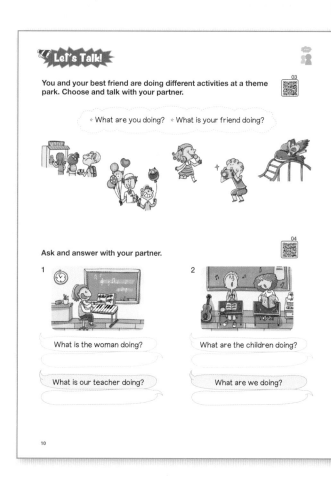

Let's Talk!

This section has two parts. The first part is designed as a conversation. It is a fun way for the students to answer a specific question as they may choose one or two answers from a selection of several choices. The second part allows the students to look at mini pictures and answer questions checking their comprehension and giving them a chance to speak.

Speak Out!

Choose one person and say two activities that the person is doing. Your classmates will guess who you are talking about.

Unit 1 We Are Playing Together 11

Unit 04

Be a Detective!

Work in pairs. Guess what each person does in the evening. Then, take turns asking your partner. The winner is the first one who completes the chart.

How to play
Q Does Finn eat dinner at 6 p.m.?
A Yes, he does. ➡ Write the number of the picture on the chart.
A No, he doesn't. ➡ Wait for the next chance.

Player 2 goes to page 78.

Player 1	John	Finn	Lily	Julie
6 p.m.				
7 p.m.				
8 p.m.				

24

Unit 01

What Are They Doing?

Flip a coin and move along the board. When you land on each space, say what the person or people are doing. Go up the snake and down the ladders.

Start

Finish

12

Speak Out!

This section is a group or class activity. It has one question and two large pictures. Each of the pictures has enough material for groups to generate different answers.

Fun Activities

This section allows the students to reinforce or expand their speaking in a fun way. Each unit has activities such as bingo, spot the differences, information gap, find a friend, and a board game. The students can relax and have fun while using English.

★ **Review Test · Teaching Materials**
free download at www.ihappyhouse.co.kr

We Are Playing Together

01

Look and talk.

1 Where are the people in the picture?

2 What are they doing?

3 Do you often go to an Internet cafe? What do you do there?

02

 **You Can Say This**   • when talking about what people or animals are doing

> The children are playing computer games.
> The man is writing an email and drinking coffee.
> The dog is sleeping on the sofa.

 **Let's Talk!**

03

You and your best friend are doing different activities at a theme park. Choose and talk with your partner.

✸ What are you doing? ✸ What is your friend doing?

04

Ask and answer with your partner.

1

What is the woman doing?

What is our teacher doing?

2

What are the children doing?

What are we doing?

 **Speak Out!**

Choose one person and say two activities that the person is doing.
Your classmates will guess who you are talking about.

1

2

What Are They Doing?

Flip a coin and move along the board. When you land on each space, say what the person or people are doing. Go up the snake and down the ladders.

+1 +2

05

Look and talk.

1 What is the girl in the picture doing?

2 What does her hair look like?

3 Does she look happy? If yes, why do you think so?

06

 **You Can Say This**

• when talking about what people look like

> The girl is tall.
> Her hair is long and blond. She has brown eyes.
> She is wearing a blue dress.
> She looks happy.

 **Let's Talk!**

Let's make an avatar! Choose two items and talk about them with your partner.

07

☆ What is your avatar wearing?

08

Ask and answer with your partner.

1

What does the boy look like?

What do I look like?

2

How does the girl look?

How do I look?

Speak Out!

Talk about the differences between the two people.

1

Jenny

Lily

2

BUS STOP

Tom

Jack

Guess Who?

Work in pairs. Choose one person. Your partner will ask you three questions to learn who the person is. The winner is the one who finds the most people.

How to play

Q Is it a man or woman?   **A** It's a man.

Q Is he wearing glasses?   **A** No.

Q Does he have blond hair?   **A** Yes.

Q Is it number 10?   **A** That's correct. / No, that's incorrect.

Shapes Are Everywhere

Look and talk.

1 What shapes of cushions can you see in the picture?

2 What colors are they?

3 Can you describe any cushions at your home?

 **You Can Say This**

• when talking about objects

> My cushion is orange.
> It is small. It looks like a star.
> It feels soft and light.

Close your eyes! Your partner will give you something. Touch it and say how it feels by using the words below. Then, guess what it is.

11

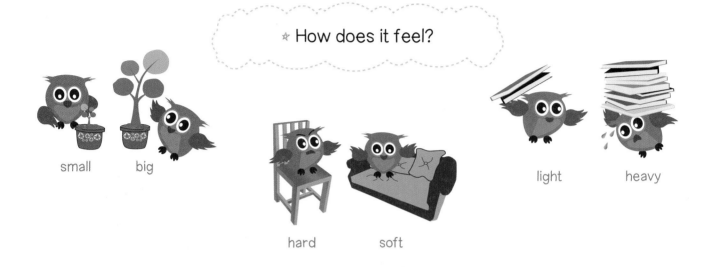

★ How does it feel?

small   big

hard   soft

light   heavy

Ask and answer with your partner.

12

1

What can you see?

What shape is the clock
in our classroom?

2

What shape can you see?

What square shapes can you
find in our classroom?

Speak Out!

Choose one object and say two things about it. Your classmates will guess which object you are talking about.

Spot the Differences

Work in pairs. Find the differences between the two pictures as fast as you can and tell your partner. The winner is the one who finds the most differences.

I Am Busy Every Day

13

Look and talk.

1 What is the girl in the picture doing?

2 What time is it?

3 Do you read books every day? When do you do that?

14

 **You Can Say This**

• when talking about daily routines

I wake up at 7:30 in the morning.
Then, I go to school with my sister.
I eat lunch at noon. After school, I go to English class.
I read books at 9 o'clock and go to bed at 10 o'clock.

Let's Talk!

What do you do every day? Choose all the activities you do and talk with your partner.

15

☆ What do you do every day?

Ask and answer with your partner.

16

1

What are the children doing?

What time do you eat breakfast?

2

What time is it?

What do you do at 6 o'clock?

Say which activities you do NOT do every day. Then, say the activities you do every day in the correct order.

1

2

Be a Detective!

Work in pairs. Guess what each person does in the evening. Then, take turns asking your partner. The winner is the first one who completes the chart.

How to play

Q Does <u>Finn</u> <u>eat dinner</u> at <u>6 p.m.</u>?

A Yes, he does. ➡ Write the number of the picture on the chart.

A No, he doesn't. ➡ Wait for the next chance.

6

1

2

3

4

5

👉 **Player 2 goes to page 86.**

👉 Player 1	John	Finn	Lily	Julie
6 p.m.	🧒	( )	🧒	( )
7 p.m.	🧒	( )	🧒	🧒
8 p.m.	( )	🧒	( )	( )

Where Is the Sofa?

17

Look and talk.

1 What rooms are in the house?

2 What is your favorite room in the house? Why?

3 Where is the sofa in the living room?

18

 **You Can Say This** • when talking about locations

> There are a sofa, a lamp, a coffee table, and a TV in the living room.
> The sofa is behind the coffee table.
> The lamp is next to the sofa. The TV is on the wall.

Make your dream bedroom! Choose three items you want to have in it and tell your partner.

19

⋆ What is in your dream bedroom?

Ask and answer with your partner.

20

1

Where are the candies and chocolates?

Where do you keep your snacks?

2

Where is the school?

What is next to your school?

Speak Out!

Talk about the locations of the person, ghosts, and other things.

1

2

Spot the Differences

Work in pairs. Find the differences between the two pictures as fast as you can and tell your partner. The winner is the one who finds the most differences.

Unit 06 I Love Animals

21

Look and talk.

1 Have you ever seen a koala in person?

2 What does a koala look like?

3 What does a koala eat?

22

 **You Can Say This**

• when talking about animals

> A koala has gray or brown fur.
> It has big ears and sharp claws.
> It lives in trees and eats leaves.
> It can sleep in trees.

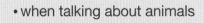

Let's Talk!

23

Animals have different homes. Choose two animals and ask your partner about their homes.

☆ Where do the animals live?

24

Ask and answer with your partner.

1

What is the horse doing?

What can horses do?

2

What does a bat look like?

What can bats do?

Say what you know about the animals.

1

2

Animal Bingo

Work in pairs. Take turns saying an animal's name and two facts about it.
Circle the animals you and your partner say. The winner is the first one who
has four circles in a row and calls out, "Bingo!"

👆 Player 1   👉 Player 2 goes to page 87.

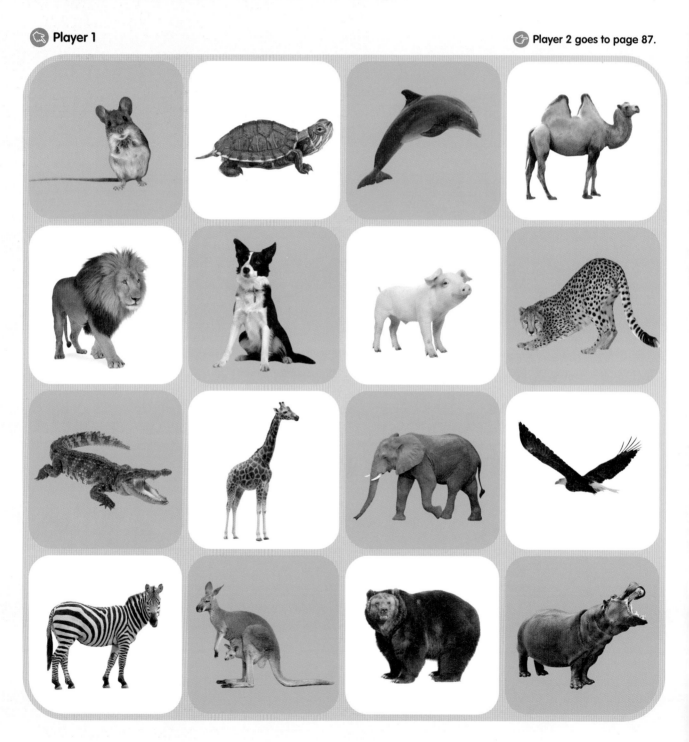

Welcome to My Neighborhood

Look and talk.

1 What buildings and places can you see in the picture?

2 Where do you think the girl is going?

3 What can you do at the post office?

You Can Say This　　　　• when talking about places in a neighborhood

• I go to the post office to mail letters.
• I can buy stamps at the post office.

 **Let's Talk!**

27

There are so many places to go in the neighborhood. Choose your favorite place and talk about it with your partner.

✦ What is your favorite place in the neighborhood? Why?

28

Ask and answer with your partner.

1

Where is the boy going?

What kinds of places are in your school?

2

Where is the girl?

What can you do at the library?

Speak Out!

Say what you can see and what the people are doing.

1

2

My Neighborhood

Flip a coin and move along the board. When you land on each space, say what the place is and what you can do there.

+1   10   +2

Do You Like All Kinds of Food?

29

Look and talk.

1 Name all the foods in the picture.

2 Which ones do you like?

3 Which ones do you NOT like? Why?

30

🍴 **You Can Say This**

• when talking about what you like or dislike

I like pizza because I like cheese.
I don't like shrimp because I have an allergy to shrimp.

 **Let's Talk!**

What kinds of movies do you like? Choose and talk with your partner. 31

☆ Which movies do you like the best?

romance

horror

action

science fiction

animation

Ask and answer with your partner. 32

1

What seasons are
in the picture?

Which season do you like,
summer or winter? Why?

2

What is happening
in the picture?

Which special day do you like,
Christmas or your birthday?
Why?

Speak Out!

Talk about which classes or pets you like and why. Then, talk about which ones you dislike and give reasons.

• Make a Choice! •

Circle the picture you like more from each pair. Ask your classmates if they like the same things you chose. The winner is the first one who completes the chart.

How to play

Q Do you like <u>pizza</u>?

A Yes, I do because ... ➡ Write their names below that picture.

A No, I don't. I like <u>chicken</u>. ➡ Ask another classmate.

That Is What I Need!

33

Look and talk.

1 What are the people in the picture doing?

2 Do you like camping? Why or why not?

3 What do you need when you go camping?

34

 **You Can Say This**

• when talking about things you need

> • I need a tent, a campfire, and food for camping.
> • I'm going camping, so I need a sleeping bag and a cap.

 **Let's Talk!**

35

Let's make a pizza! What do you need for toppings? Choose three things and talk with your partner.

✧ What toppings do you need for your pizza?

36

Ask and answer with your partner.

1

What is the boy thinking about?

What do you need when you have a birthday party?

2

What is the girl thinking about?

What do you need when you go to the beach?

**Choose the items you need to do something and say their names.
Your classmates will guess what you are going to do with them.**

1

2

What's the Problem?

Flip a coin and move along the board. When you land on each space, say what the person or people need.

+1   +2

Unit 10 Sometimes I Feel Annoyed

Look and talk.

1 What is happening in the picture?

2 How does the girl look?

3 When do you feel annoyed?

 **You Can Say This**

• when talking about feelings

> I feel annoyed when my sister eats my food.
> I feel happy when I have no homework.
> I feel sad when it is raining on picnic day.

Let's Talk!

When do you feel scared? Choose and tell your partner.

39

> ✸ When do you feel scared?

Ask and answer with your partner.

40

1

> How does the boy look?

> How do you feel when you are home alone? Why?

2

> What is happening in the picture?

> Do you feel happy when you visit your grandparents? Why or why not?

Talk about what is happening and how the person or people feel. Then, talk about when you feel the same way.

1

2

My Feelings

Flip a coin and move along the board. When you land on each picture, say when you feel that way. When you land on each expression, say how you feel at that time.

+1 +2

This Is My Family

41

Look and talk.

1 Who is in this family?

2 Do you have any brothers or sisters? If yes, what are they like?

3 What do your parents like?

42

  • when talking about people around you

> My dad is a police officer. He likes music.
> My mom is a teacher. She loves yoga.
> My brother is funny, and he is good at art.

 Let's Talk!

What kind of person are you? Choose and talk with your partner.

quiet

* What are you like?

talkative

funny

kind

cheerful

Ask and answer with your partner.

44

1

What is the boy good at?

Can any of your friends dance really well? Who are they?

2

What is the girl good at?

What subject are you good at?

Speak Out!

In the first picture, match each person with a job and a hobby and talk about them. In the second picture, match each person with a personality and an ability and talk about them.

1

2

Find a Friend!

Ask your classmates and learn who matches with each picture. Then, write his or her name below each picture. The winner is the one who has the most names.

Let's Imagine!

Look and talk.

1 What is happening in the picture?

2 Where is the girl flying to?

3 Imagine you can fly. What would you do?

 **You Can Say This** • when talking about imaginary situations

- I would fly to Australia.
- I would be a superhero and help people.
- I would sleep on a cloud in the sky.

Let's Talk!

Imagine you can have a superpower. Choose and talk with your partner.

47

* What would your superpower be?   * What would you do with it?

super smart

super strong

super fast

super tall

48

Ask and answer with your partner.

1

Why is the man happy?

Imagine you have a lot of money. What would you do?

2

What is happening in the picture?

Imagine you are a dog. What would you do?

Talk about what is happening. Then, imagine you are the girl or boy and talk about what you would do.

1

2

Imagination Is Fun

Flip a coin and move along the board. When you land on each space, imagine that happens to you and say what you would do.

+1   (5)   (10)   +2

Start

You turn into a monster.

+1

You can control the weather.

You have a robot.

-2

You can change your face.

You turn into your mom.

You are as small as a mouse.

-1

You turn into a teacher.

Finish

My Pet Is Sick

Look and talk.

1 What is this place?

2 What is the woman's job?

3 When do you go to the animal hospital?

 **You Can Say This**

• when talking about jobs

> Vets help sick animals.
> They give medicine to sick animals.
> They work at animal hospitals.
> They wear a uniform. They are very kind.

You have a chance for your dream job. Choose and talk with your partner.

51

> ✦ What is your dream job?　✦ What does a person with that job do?

52

Ask and answer with your partner.

1

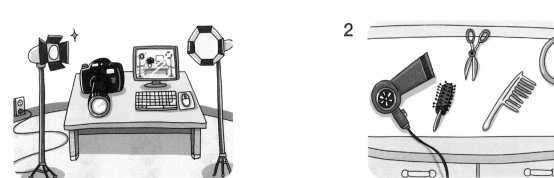

Where can you see these things?

What does a photographer do?

2

Who uses these things?

When do you go to a hair salon?

Speak Out!

Talk about what is strange in the pictures.

1

2

Job World

Flip a coin and move along the board. When you land on each space, say things about the job.

+1 +2

Unit 14 What Will Happen Next?

Look and talk.

1 What is happening in the pictures?

2 Imagine you see many UFOs coming. How would you feel?

3 What do you think will happen next?

 **You Can Say This** • when talking about what you think will happen

- I think lots of scary aliens will come out.
- I expect cute and friendly aliens will come out.
- Perhaps the UFOs will take all the people and fly away.

Uh-oh! The teacher turned into a gorilla. Choose what you think will happen next and talk with your partner.

55

★ What will happen next?

Ask and answer with your partner.

56

1 What is happening in the pictures?

2 What do you think will happen next?

Look and think about what will happen next. Then, tell your own story by using the pictures.

• What Will Happen Next? •

**Make groups. Read each story and answer the questions together.
Then, share the best ending from your group with your classmates.**

Ashley is asleep in bed. Her mother shouts, "Time for school!
You are late!" Ashley jumps out of bed. She eats breakfast
quickly and then washes her face. She brushes her teeth
and gets on the school bus.
Everyone on the bus looks at Ashley and starts
laughing. Ashley is in her pajamas!

1 What does Ashley do after she wakes up?

2 Why do Ashley's friends laugh at her?

3 What do you think will happen next?

There is a little boy who has a pet dragon. The dragon has a cave with lots
of treasure. A witch living in the woods wants the dragon's treasure.
One day, the boy flies high up in the sky on his dragon.
Suddenly, the witch is following them on her broom!
She starts to say a magic spell and then...

1 What is the boy doing?

2 Why does the witch follow the boy and the dragon?

3 What do you think will happen next?

Let's Twist Fairy Tales!

Look and talk.

1 Who is Cinderella dancing with?

2 Imagine you are Cinderella. Would you leave the glass shoe?

3 What do you think will happen next?

 **You Can Say This**   • when talking about what you think will happen

• I think the prince will marry the ugly sister.
• I expect Cinderella will grab the glass shoe and try it on.
• Perhaps Cinderella will find another prince.

The girl is asking for help. Choose what you think will happen next and talk with your partner.

61

✶ What do you think the prince will do?

62

Ask and answer with your partner.

1 What is happening in the pictures?

2 What do you think will happen next?

Look and think about what will happen next. Then, tell your own story by using the pictures.

What Will Happen Next?

Make groups. Read each story and answer the questions together. Then, share the best ending from your group with your classmates.

Three little pigs build their own houses. One pig makes a house out of chocolate. One pig makes a house out of cheese, and the last pig makes a house out of pizza. A big, scary wolf walks by and sees the houses. He says, "Let me in, or I will eat your houses!" All the pigs run away. The wolf eats the chocolate house, the cheese house, and the pizza house. Then, he sees the pigs hiding in the forest.

1 What kinds of houses do the pigs make?

2 What does the wolf do to the pigs' houses?

3 What do you think will happen next?

There is a beautiful mermaid princess. She helps a prince who falls into the ocean. She falls in love with the prince, but she is a mermaid. Mermaids live in the ocean. The mermaid princess does a magic spell to turn the prince into a merman. Suddenly, he grows a long fishy tail and can swim fast.

1 How do the mermaid princess and the prince meet?

2 Why does the mermaid princess turn the prince into a merman?

3 What do you think will happen next?

Unit 16 Which Side Are You On?

Look and talk.

1 Do you have any pets? What are they?

2 If you don't have a pet, which pet do you want?

3 Many people think dogs make better pets than cats. What do you think?

 **You Can Say This** • when talking about your opinions

> • I agree because dogs are more fun and friendlier.
> • I disagree because dogs are loud but cats are quiet.
> • I don't think so. I don't like walking the dog.

Let's Talk!

What is your favorite season? Choose and ask your partner if he or she agrees.

67

> ☆ The best season of the year is this. Do you agree?

Ask and answer with your partner.

68

1 How do the places in the pictures look?

2 Which is better to live in and why?

Tell your partner what you think and ask if he or she agrees.

Say which statement you agree with and why. Write down the names of your classmates who are on the same side as you.

1

Ice cream is better than fruit.

Fruit is better than ice cream.

2

The beach is better than the park.

The park is better than the beach.

Let's Debate!

Read and debate.

How to debate

1 Read the statement and take a side.

2 Make teams with students who are on the same side.

3 Brainstorm reasons why you agree or disagree. Then, write them down.

4 Now, the debate begins! The two teams take turns saying one reason at a time. The winner is the team that has the most reasons.

Day is better than night.

Agree

Disagree

Wearing a school uniform is better than wearing everyday clothes.

Agree

Disagree

Appendices

Key Words

Unit 01

play computer games

wait for tickets

buy a balloon

take pictures

rollercoaster

play the piano

sing

cap

escalator

talk on the phone

sunglasses

shopping bags

Unit 02

blond

glasses

dress

basketball jersey

sweatshirt

excited

angry

tired

scared

beard

bald

upset

Unit 03

square

circle

star

heart

clock

plate

coin

full moon

tent

kite

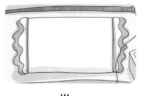

pillow

cellphone

Unit 04

by bus

play soccer

wash the dishes

eat breakfast

paint

put out fires

brush my teeth

get dressed

go to bed

do my homework

play the harp

take a shower

Unit 05

fridge

bench

in the tree

on the swings

a dog next to the girl

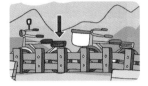
behind the fence

in the bookcase

under the bed

behind the computer

a picture on the wall

a cap on the floor

a lamp next to the bed

Unit 06

doghouse

bird nest

pond

wing

polar bear

seal

rabbit

have long ears

like carrots

under the ground

eat grass

dig

Unit 07

pet store

bookstore

toy store

cinema

playground

vegetables

fruits

wait in line

chef

take an order

order food

serve food

Unit 08

corn

broccoli

shrimp

summer

fall

taekwondo

math

Chinese

kitten

parrot

goldfish

turtle

Unit 09

pineapple

olive

swimsuit

swimming tube

blanket

glove

toothbrush

toothpaste

soil

shovel

map

wrapping paper

Unit 10

have a bad dream

watch a horror movie

ride a Viking ship

thunderstorm

look worried

visit her grandparents

proud

annoyed

angry

sad

bored

embarrassed

Unit 11

quiet

talkative

cheerful

good at dancing

doctor

play the guitar

play badminton

shop

shy

smart

lazy

art

Unit 12

fly

surf

Australia

super smart

super strong

super fast

won the lottery

turned into a dog

see a monster

can't see him

control the weather

change your face

Unit 13

vet

model

actor

pro-gamer

president

firefighter

pilot

magician

police officer

cut the carrot with a brush

nurse

dentist

Unit 14

UFO

alien

run away

play with the gorilla

teach

throw

a glass on the table

meet some little fairies

a tiny door in the tree

change her into a small girl

laugh

dragon

Unit 15

dance

leave the glass shoe

magic flying carpet

ladder

fly a helicopter to her

walk away

witch

make an apple pie

castle

beast

change into a prince

mermaid

Unit 16

pets

spring

winter

city

country

ice cream

beach

park

day

night

school uniform

everyday clothes

Talk Some More 1

Roll a die and move along the board.
Answer the questions or talk about the pictures.

START

Imagine you are a bird. What would you do?

Find something long and thin.

What do you need when you go hiking?

What do you do before you go to school?

Say Anyting

Miss a Turn

Talk about yourself.

Who is sitting next to you?

When do you feel annoyed?

Do you like spicy food? Why or why not?

When do you go to the hospital?

What does your pet look like?

2 km

Talk Some More 2

Roll a die and move along the board. Answer the questions or talk about the pictures. Go down the snakes.

START

Describe your bag.

Talk about your pet.

When do you feel excited?

Who is sitting in front of you?

What time do you go to bed?

Where do you live?

Find three circles in your classroom.

What sport are you good at?

What does a firefighter do?

Talk about your teacher.

Do you like long hair? Why or why not?

Name two things you do NOT like.

What does your dad look like?

Find a person who likes vegetables.

Do you like going to the zoo? Why or why not?

Ho do y feel r

How do you feel when you get up early on Saturday?

Name three things that are red.

What does a panda look like?

Do you agree that summer is better than winter? Why or why not?

Imagine you are a superhero. What would you do?

Name two animals that have wings.

Do you feel happy when you go to school?

Do you like camping? Why or why not?

How does a teddy bear feel?

When do you go to the post office?

When do you feel upset?

Who is your favorite singer?

What do you need when you go swimming?

What are you doing?

FINISH

Be a Detective!

Work in pairs. Guess what each person does in the evening. Then, take turns asking your partner. The winner is the first one who completes the chart.

How to play

Q Does <u>Finn</u> <u>eat dinner</u> at <u>6 p.m.</u>?

A Yes, he does. ➡ Write the number of the picture on the chart.

A No, he doesn't. ➡ Wait for the next chance.

👉 Player 2	John	Finn	Lily	Julie
6 p.m.	( )		( )	
7 p.m.	( )		( )	( )
8 p.m.		( )		

Animal Bingo

Work in pairs. Take turns saying an animal's name and two facts about it. Circle the animals you and your partner say. The winner is the first one who has four circles in a row and calls out, "Bingo!"

Player 2

Talk to Me

Workbook

2ND Edition

1

Happy House

Talk to Me 2ND Edition to Me 1

Workbook

Happy House

Contents

Picture Description

Picture Discussion

We Are Playing Together

A Write the correct words for the pictures.

cap   escalator   shopping bag   sing   sunglasses   rollercoaster

1

_____

2

_____

3

_____

4

_____

5

_____

6

_____

B Look and write.

1

Q What are you doing?

A I am e_____ ice cream.

2

Q What are they doing?

A They are p_____ computer games.

C Unscramble and write the sentences.

1

pictures. / taking / is / My friend

_____

2

waiting for / tickets. / I'm

_____

D Complete the sentences using the words in the box.

| baby   down   music   talking |

1 The person ❶ is holding a crying _____.

2 The person ❷ is _____ on the phone.

3 The person ❸ is going _____ the escalator and listening to

_____ .

02 Everyone Looks Different

A Write the correct words for the pictures.

| glasses | blond | tired | dress | basketball jersey | sweatshirt |

1

_____

2

_____

3

_____

4

_____

5

_____

6

_____

B Look and write.

1

The man has short b_____ hair.

He has a b_____.

2

The man is b_____.

He has b_____ eyes.

C Read and match.

| What does the boy look like? | • | • | He is tall. He has short green hair. |

| How does the girl look? | • | • | She looks sad. |

D Look and write T for true or F for false.

1 Jenny is tall, but Lily is short. (   )

2 Jenny has long red hair, but Lily has short brown hair. (   )

3 Jenny looks angry, but Lily looks excited. (   )

Shapes Are Everywhere

A Write the correct words for the pictures.

| square   circle   star   heart   tent   kite |

1

_____

2

_____

3

_____

4

_____

5

_____

6

_____

B Look and write.

1

Q How does it feel?

A It is h_____.

2

Q How does it feel?

A It is s_____.

C Unscramble and write the sentences.

1

a circle. / The clock / looks like

_____

2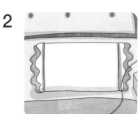

is / light and soft. / The pillow

_____

D Complete the sentences using the words in the box.

| circle   picnic mat   blue   diamond |

1 The kite is orange and _____. It looks like a _____.

2 The beachball is light. It looks like a _____.

3 The _____ is light. It is white and yellow.

A Write the correct words for the pictures.

wash the dishes   put out fires   paint   get dressed   go to bed   take a shower

1

2

3

_____

_____

_____

4

5

6

_____

_____

_____

B Look and write.

1

Q What do you do every day?

A I go to school b_____ bus.

2

Q What do you do every day?

A I play s_____.

C Read and match.

What time do you eat breakfast? •

• It is 6 o'clock.

What time is it? •

• I eat breakfast at 7 o'clock.

D Match the pictures with the correct sentences.

1

2

3

4

• I brush my teeth.

• I eat breakfast.

• I go to school.

• I do my homework.

Unit 05 Where Is the Sofa?

A Write the correct words for the pictures.

| lamp | bed | sofa | TV | window | fridge |

1

_____

2

_____

3

_____

4

_____

5

_____

6

_____

B Look and write.

1

Q Where are the candies and chocolates?

A They are u_____ the cookies and cupcakes.

2

Q Where is the school?

A It is b_____ the hospital and the police station.

12

C Unscramble and write the sentences.

1  behind / is / The sofa / the coffee table.

_____

2 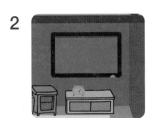 is / the wall. / The TV / on

_____

D Complete the sentences using the words in the box.

| behind | in | under | bookcase |

1 ❶: There is a ghost _____ the _____.

2 ❷: There is a ghost _____ the bed.

3 ❸: There is a ghost _____ the computer.

I Love Animals

A Write the correct words for the pictures.

pond   wing   polar bear   seal   doghouse   bird nest

1

_____

2

_____

3

_____

4

_____

5

_____

6

_____

B Look and write.

1

Q Where do whales live?

A Whales live in the o_____.

2

Q Where do monkeys live?

A Monkeys live in t_____.

C Read and match.

What can horses do? •

• A bat has long ears and claws.

What does a bat look like? •

• Horses can run fast.

D Look and write T for true or F for false.

1 ❶: Rabbits have short ears and long tails. (   )

2 ❷: Rabbits eat grass. (   )

3 ❸: Rabbits like carrots. (   )

A Write the correct words for the pictures.

| cinema | toy store | playground | pet store | bookstore | fruits |

1

_____

2

_____

3

_____

4

_____

5

_____

6

_____

B Look and write.

1

Q Where is the boy going?

A He is going to s_____.

2

Q Where is the girl?

A She is in the l_____.

C Unscramble and write the sentences.

1

a cart. / The woman / is pushing

_____

2

The woman / is holding / a shopping basket.

_____

D Complete the sentences using the words in the box.

| order   food   chef   cooking |

1 ❶: The _____ is _____.

2 ❷: A waiter is taking an _____.

3 ❸: Some people are ordering _____.

Do You Like All Kinds of Food?

A Write the correct words for the pictures.

corn   broccoli   shrimp   math   Chinese   parrot

1

_____

2

_____

3

_____

4

_____

5

_____

6

_____

B Look and write.

1

Q Which movies do you like the best?

A I like a_____ movies.

2

Q Which movies do you like the best?

A I like s_____ f_____ movies.

C Read and match.

> Which season do you like, summer or winter? Why?

> I like my birthday because all my friends give me gifts.

> Which special day do you like, Christmas or your birthday? Why?

> I like summer because I can have fun at the beach.

D Match the pictures with the correct sentences.

1

I like art because I am good at drawing.

2

I don't like kittens because they have sharp claws.

3

I don't like turtles because they are boring.

4

I like goldfish because they are fun to watch.

That Is What I Need!

A Write the correct words for the pictures.

| swimsuit | swimming tube | olive | pineapple | blanket | glove |

1

_____

2

_____

3

_____

4

_____

5

_____

6

_____

B Look and write.

1

Q What toppings do you need for your pizza?

A I need m_____.

2

Q What do you need when you go camping?

A I need a t_____ and food for camping.

C Unscramble and write the sentences.

1  going to the beach. / She / is thinking about

_____

2  a birthday cake / need / I / for the party.

_____

D Complete the sentences using the words in the box.

baseball   helmet   soil

1 ❶: I need a bike and a _____.

2 ❷: I need some _____ and a shovel.

3 ❸: I need a glove and a _____.

Sometimes I Feel Annoyed

A Write the correct words for the pictures.

sad Viking ship thunderstorm horror movie spider annoyed

1

_____

2

_____

3

_____

4

_____

5

_____

6

_____

B Look and write.

1

Q When do you feel scared?

A I feel scared when I have a bad d_____.

2

Q How does the boy look?

A He looks w_____.

C Read and match.

When do you feel annoyed?

I feel annoyed when my sister eats my food.

How do you feel when you are home alone?

I feel scared.

D Look and write T for true or F for false.

1 There are five boys. (   )

2 They won the basketball championship. (   )

3 They feel sad. (   )

This Is My Family

A Write the correct words for the pictures.

> quiet   talkative   cheerful   doctor   shop   shy

1

_____

2

_____

3

_____

4

_____

5

_____

6

_____

B Look and write.

1

Q What are you like?

A I am f_____.

2

Q What are you like?

A I am k_____.

C Unscramble and write the sentences.

1

He / dancing. / is good at

_____

2

a teacher. / My mom / is

_____

D Match the pictures with the correct sentences.

1

•   • (She is smart.)

2

•   • (He likes playing badminton.)

3

•   • (She is lazy.)

4

•   • (He likes playing the guitar.)

Let's Imagine!

A Write the correct words for the pictures.

| fly | surf | Australia | super fast | won the lottery | can't see him |

1

_____

2

_____

3

_____

4

_____

5

_____

6

_____

B Look and write.

1

Q What would your superpower be?

A I would be s_____ s_____.

2

Q What would your superpower be?

A I would be s_____ s_____.

C Read and match.

Imagine you have
a lot of money.
What would you do? •

• I would sleep on a
cloud in the sky.

Imagine you can fly.
What would you do? •

• I would buy a big house.

D Look and write T for true or F for false.

1 The girl sees a monster. (   )

2 She looks happy. (   )

3 The monster is on her bed. (   )

A Write the correct words for the pictures.

> hair dryer   brush   dentist   nurse   model   actor

1

_____

2

_____

3

_____

4

_____

5

_____

6

_____

B Look and write.

1

Q What does a vet do?

A A vet helps sick a_____.

2

Q What does a president do?

A A president takes care of the c_____.

C Unscramble and write the sentences.

1

plays / A pro-gamer / computer games.

_____

2

A photographer / people, places, or things. / takes pictures of

_____

D Complete the sentences using the words in the box.

| police   windows   magician   putting out |

1 ❶: The firefighter is cleaning the _____.

2 ❷: The pilot is _____ the fire.

3 ❸: The _____ is driving a _____ car.

What Will Happen Next?

A Write the correct words for the pictures.

> fairy   throw   laugh   alien   dragon   UFO

1

_____

2

_____

3

_____

4

_____

5

_____

6

_____

B Match the pictures with the correct sentences.

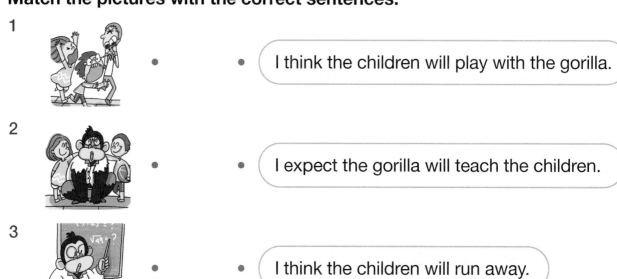

1

     I think the children will play with the gorilla.

2

     I expect the gorilla will teach the children.

3

     I think the children will run away.

C Match the number in the picture to the correct sentence.

1 _____ The little girl says, "I want to go inside." The fairies change her into a small girl.

2 _____ A little girl is walking in the forest. She meets some little fairies.

3 _____ The little fairies take her to a tree. There is a tiny door in the tree.

4 _____ The fairies fly over to her. They say, "Come with us."

D Look and write.

gets on   asleep   laughing   breakfast

Ashley is _____ in bed. Her mother shouts, "Time for school! You are late!"

Ashley jumps out of bed. She eats _____ quickly and then washes her face.

She brushes her teeth and _____ the school bus.

Everyone on the bus looks at Ashley and starts _____ .

Ashley is in her pajamas!

Unit 15 Let's Twist Fairy Tales!

A Write the correct words for the pictures.

> beast   mermaid   dance   witch   castle   helicopter

1  _____

2  _____

3  _____

4  _____

5  _____

6  _____

B Match the pictures with the correct sentences.

1 • • I think the prince will use a magic flying carpet.

2 • • Perhaps the prince will walk away.

3  • • I think the prince will bring a ladder and save he

C Match the number in the picture to the correct sentence.

1 _____ She kisses the beast.

2 _____ The beast doesn't change into a prince.

3 _____ The beautiful girl thinks the beast will change into a prince.

4 _____ There is a beast in a castle.

D Look and write.

> tail   love   helps   merman

There is a beautiful mermaid princess. She _____ a prince who falls into the ocean. She falls in _____ with the prince, but she is a mermaid. Mermaids live in the ocean. The mermaid princess does a magic spell to turn the prince into a _____. Suddenly, he grows a long fishy _____ and can swim fast.

Unit 16 Which Side Are You On?

A Write the correct words for the pictures.

> spring   winter   school uniform   night   pets   ice cream

1

_____

2

_____

3

_____

4

_____

5

_____

6

_____

B Unscramble and write the sentences.

1

The beach is better than the park because

at the beach. / can swim / we

The beach is better than the park because

_____

2

The park is better than the beach because

I / there. / my bike / can ride

The park is better than the beach because

_____

C Read and match.

I think fall is the best season of the year. Do you agree? •

• I want a rabbit.

If you don't have a pet, which pet do you want? •

• Yes, I agree.

D Complete the sentences using the words in the box.

> calm   busy   because

1 The city looks very _____.

2 The country looks _____ and quiet.

3 I want to live in the city _____ I can go anywhere on a bus or subway.

Key Sentences Review

Look and write.

1 (1)

Q What are you doing?

A I am e_____ ice cream.

(2)

Q What are they doing?

A They are p_____ computer games.

2 (1)

The man has short b_____ hair.

He has a b_____.

(2)

The man is b_____.

He has b_____ eyes.

3 (1)

Q How does it feel?

A It is h_____.

(2)

Q How does it feel?

A It is s_____.

4 (1)

Q What do you do every day?

A I go to school b_____ bus.

(2)

Q What do you do every day?

A I play s_____.

5 (1)

Q Where are the candies and chocolates?

A They are u_____ the cookies and cupcakes.

(2)

Q Where is the school?

A It is b_____ the hospital and the police station.

6 (1)

Q Where do whales live?

A Whales live in the o_____.

(2)

Q Where do monkeys live?

A Monkeys live in t_____.

7 (1)

Q Where is the boy going?

A He is going to s_____.

(2)

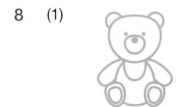

Q Where is the girl?

A She is in the l_____.

8 (1)

Q Which movies do you like the best?

A I like a_____ movies.

(2)

Q Which movies do you like the best?

A I like s_____ f_____ movies.

9 (1)

Q What toppings do you need for your pizza?

A I need m_____.

(2)

Q What do you need when you go camping?

A I need a t_____ and food for camping.

10 (1)

Q When do you feel scared?

A I feel scared when I have a bad d_____.

(2)

Q How does the boy look?

A He looks w_____.

11 (1)

Q What are you like?

A I am f_____.

(2)

Q What are you like?

A I am k_____.

12 (1)

Q What would your superpower be?

A I would be s_____ s_____.

(2)

Q What would your superpower be?

A I would be s_____ s_____.

13 (1)

Q What does a vet do?

A A vet helps sick a_____.

(2)

Q What does a president do?

A A president takes care of the c_____.

14 (1)

The beach is better than the park because

<u>at the beach. / can swim / we</u>

The beach is better than the park because

_____

(2)

The park is better than the beach because

<u>I / there. / my bike / can ride</u>

The park is better than the beach because

_____

Talk to Me 1

2ND Edition

Workbook

• Components •
Student Book / Workbook

• Online Resources •
eBook, Audio Files, Lesson Plan, Answer Key, Word List, Test Sheets, PPTs, and others